SHIMA (Isl

Tamiko Dooley

abuddhapress@yahoo.com

ISBN: 9798361830602

for my first piano teacher, Lisa Childs, who taught me how to play

HOKKAIDO

Shikii (Tracks)

I stood in the doorway
You had removed your slippers
Left them in the corridor

You were gliding Across the *tatami* floor
Towards the dining table
Where I once laid out *hojicha* tea

You warmed your feet
On the *kotatsu* under The blanket
Closed your eyes

You couldn't see me

I was sliding back and forth
Fusing with the paper *fusuma* doors
Immovable horizontal Tracks

Unable to move forwards towards you
Join you at the table
Couldn't travel back to the front door
Leading to the world I left behind

I stood in the doorway

I was sliding

You couldn't

Shinrin-yoku (Forest bathing)

You were turned away in Tetsugaku-dou Park
I saw you hunched over

I was bathing myself in the greenery
Crickets hummed shriller the deeper I rambled

Your outline in the foliage was unmistakeable
Stooping, the way you used to when examining a seedling

The scent of the soil was heady and musty
I tried to call out your name

It was lost in the undergrowth
Seeds carried to another forest to be reborn

As I crept closer
Your shape gave way to leaves and branches

And when I reached out to touch you

My fingers brushed against stems
As gentle as the droplets of rain that stained my cheeks

Toshokan (Library)

I heard your voice
Technicolour tones on a grey day
Ringing through my body

I'd only been browsing
Picking up the third book I was drawn to
Fingers tracing the letters on the cover

That was when it happened

I knew it was you on the page
You were smiling
Telling me that I could keep going

I felt your hand on my shoulder
A *manatsu* moon glowing above me
Pushing the clouds aside

When my tears blurred the words

I knew it was you

I'd only been browsing

I heard your voice

Quicksand

I saw you on Furusato shore
Walking away as the sun set behind us
Low tide in the early evening

We had traipsed and slid down over rolling dunes of stones
Washed up after travelling for days

You were already far ahead of me
Pale grey clouds were hanging so low
You seemed to be knocking your head on them

I tried to catch up but the
Sand kept sinking from under me
Toes splaying to keep me steady
In the murky shallow waters

The wind grabbed my hat
I reached behind me to catch it as it flew
When I turned back
In that time you had gone

My eyes scanned the horizon
Only seagulls disturbed my eyeline
Circling, calling, paddling across the seabed

When the sun disappeared
It was time to return to the beach
Where kitesurfers laid their sails to rest
Between trails of seaweed shrivelled by the *hachigatsu* sun

I took one last glance back towards the sea

It was low tide

You were walking away

I saw you on Furusato shore

Anagram

I was standing in your garden
Next to the rippling water fountain you built

Stones gathered from across Nakano prefecture during your walks
Balancing without cement
Relying on each other for support

When I would watch you construct it
You told me your *himitsu*:
To listen to where the next rock should be placed

I traced out the word "listen" in the soil
Index finger and nail discoloured
You helped me wash it off in the *ofuro*

We would sit together on the back porch
Eating shaved ice smothered in *yuzu* syrup
You would tell the story of each stone you collected
Steps on your journey

I was standing in your garden
Ten years since you left

The rocks never moved, never toppled
Kept each other upright

Everything had changed: *kawatta*
Nothing had changed: *kawaranakatta*

When I searched the ground
The letters had rearranged themselves

Spelling "silent"

Kintsugi

If you'd shown your cracks
We could have mended with gold
Held you together

wareta basho
kin de naoseta yo
kimi no jin sei

KYUSHU

First bite

I watched you gently unwrap the paper and bite the end of your cone

Chocolate-heavy, wafer tip

You tilted your head back and sucked through the matcha ice-cream

It tastes sweeter from the other end you smiled, adjusting your sunglasses

And my seventeen-year-old lilac-painted toes

Squirmed and dug deeper into the tide-soaked sand

As waves crashed inside me and against Odaiba shore

Heatstroke

you caught the sun today, you said

raising your sunglasses and examining my cheeks

your left thumb brushed under my eyes

with a touch as soft

and close as if

your lips had grazed

my collarbone

behind me the kites soared
in the sky

Tokeru (Melting)

you watched me catch with my tongue
the drips that threatened to
slither down the cone onto my hand
and laughed, *kimi ga waratta*

ahead kite surfers and jet skis roared across the Okinawa skyline
the Pacific tide was creeping towards our toes
waves pounding the shore louder and closer

and when you leaned towards me and
licked a drop of my matcha ice-cream
to save it falling

the icy fingers of the *umi* gripped my legs

Jishin (Earthquake)

I started the earthquake / *ore ga jishin* / I was lying on the futon / *asa no yoji*, four in the morning / I turned to my side / watched your chest rise and fall / outside the Tokyo rainfall began to crescendo / smacking against the Okura Hotel window / glass floor to ceiling / *kaminari* flashing across the sky / the lightbulb above our heads began to swing / a pendulum stretching higher and further / until the walls began to shudder / trembles vibrating to the core / when I reached out to wake you / take us somewhere safe / I was motionless / *ugoke nakatta* / couldn't touch your body / cracks between us: hidden, silent / I couldn't / I reached / I turned / I was lying / *ore ga jishin* / I started the earthquake

Red flags

I brushed past
You smiled
I glanced
We joked
You poured
We drank
You asked
I gave
Your lips
My coat

You rang
I agreed
We ate
You paid
I thanked
We danced
Your hands
My waist
Your flat
We lay
Your fingertips
My hair
We adored

You bought
I wore
You preferred
I stopped
You laughed
I apologised
You refused
I accepted
You demanded
I obeyed
You unpicked
I unravelled
I left, I left, I left

SHIKOKU

Hanabi (Fireworks)

Gunshots woke me
Firing into the clouds
Smoke through fog
Lights exploding

When I ran to the *mado*
To be dazzled by dappled rainbows

They stopped

Each time I slid open the bamboo shutter
Pressed my nose to the mosquito netting:

A silent, starless night
shizuka de kurai yoru

Only when I returned to my futon
Laid down my head
Would they start again

If I return to my *yume*
Will I be a part of them
Or will I be shut inside

As *hanabi* entertain
Out there

Elevator

She faces the buttons.

Going up, Floor 34.
The uniform hat perches on her slick and gleaming bun:
Regulation size.
Regulation lipstick, regulation gloves, regulation heels
(they measure them in the morning).

If you ask how often
A hand brushed against the back of her skirt
(regulation length)
Or fingers lingered on her waist
(regulation width)
She'd hide her teeth with her hand
cock her head to the side

If she hears another joke about pressing her buttons
Or how the business is going
(It has its ups and downs)
her shoulders will shake
With the laughter that bounces off four glass walls

But at night, after a bath she shares with three generations
In a cramped apartment a train ride away
Where they turn off the lights to save the yen

Her fingers grip the futon

When she closes her eyes she goes up and down
Inner ear confusing movement with memory

And as she sleeps, her teeth clench and unclench
Buttons pressed over and over
Grinding against each other in protest
Until they wear each other down over time
And nothing remains.

Spectacles

I thought you looked funny before
She said, tilting her head to one side
But now that you wear glasses
You look even funnier

The lollipop in her mouth
Moved to the other cheek
To give one side relief from the sugar.

Facts stated without irony, guilt or doubt, she skipped off to hold her aunt's hand.

The crowds pressed in on us
At Tokyo Disneyland
We could hardly move for people
Row after row of black hair and long socks
And pleated skirts, taken for a day trip

And I, a tall nine-year-old, in jeans and
Chestnut locks and frames I'd spent hours
Agonising over at the optician's

had never

felt

more

alone

Saisho to Saigo (The beginning and the end)

You were sharing a room
With the other girls
First job, first flight
Out of Narita.

6 hats perched on the tables for tomorrow,
6 skirts hanging and 6
Pairs of heels by the bolted door,
Next to the mini-fridge.

First night away from home.

Your stomach rumbled and
You remembered my grandmother
Had made you an *omusubi* rice ball
You crept out of bed to unzip your suitcase
Whilst the others shouted at you to be quiet

You unwrapped the delicate paper
Still smelling of the house in Nakano
Lines of Baba's palm molded onto the
Seaweed, her thumbprints in the rice
Signature sweet and tangy *umeboshi* at the centre

You knew then what you were leaving behind
That adventures would begin to unfold

Your tears fell silently
Blending into freshly-washed hair
Ready for tomorrow's early call
First job, first flight.

Tabi (Journey)

You travelled
12 hours by plane
6 hours by bus and taxi
Endured jet lag and security queues
Hung around in the waiting room
Screams from the two-year-old left behind
Ring in your ears

When you approach her bed
Clutching a tin of biscuits and station flowers

She asks *why are you here*
And stares out the window unsmiling

What she means is

I am so moved by your coming to see me
I have no words

If I look at you I will start crying
And never stop

I Swear

In the playground

They ask me

How many bad words I know

In my other language

Not any?

None. Zero.

They get bored of asking

Learning a language

Only from your mother

Has its

downsides

HONSHU

Gomennasai (Sorry)

She warms the water in the pan.
A tilt -
and it sizzles.
Soft blue flame
Rising against the metal saucepan
As stainless and sharp as
Her tongue.

The leaves of *hojicha* tea
Sit huddled in the cup, shoulders hunched,
Hurt,
In the cold afternoon of the kitchen.
Shafts of orange light pierce us through the
Holes torn in the paper *shoji*
Reminding us that the day's nearly done.
She takes the water threatening to bubble
off the heat just in time
and pours a towering waterfall
Expertly - nothing spills.

Not a bag, but loose leaves.
An extravagance of sorts for us,
Another way she's showing remorse.

She stirs, and each clink of the spoon
Is an apology. It turns and turns
And with each rotation it whispers

Gomen, gomen, gomen

Until she brings the cup to the table
And places it silently before me.
We both know what she means.

My hands begin to warm and soften against
The brittle ceramic.
On its underside is engraved:
Delicate treatment required.

The Arrival

I saw you waving at me
On tiptoes on an upturned trunk
You'd dragged to Nakano station
At the back of the crowded platform
You were calling my name frantically
Sunshine in your voice

When I managed to sift through the reunions
In my stiff navy brass-buttoned uniform to reach you
Your arms grabbed mine
And our tears began to wash the pain
And the shame that stained my skin

To forget, to forgive, to return

Conversation with a parent (*Ryoshin to no kaiwa*)

I told you the news
A ring, as promise of love
You wept, now alone

kimi ni yutta
ai no yubiwa da
namida dake

Motherhood

You asked me to write you a poem about *hasamimushi*

So here it is. Despite knowing

Little about earwigs

Nor liking them

(and I'm not convinced you do either)

I am writing it anyway

Because you asked me to.

Taiyo (Sunshine)

On a bright autumnal afternoon
When the sun's behind me
And my back begins to warm

I think of you
kimi omoidasu

That shaft of afternoon light
That used to reach the middle of your bedsheets
Miyazaki house, single dorm
Your desk lumbered with
Tacitus and Virgil, Sallust and Homer

On a Friday when double Greek was done
I'd find you there
Eyes closed, smiling
Your skin glowing

I'd lean in towards you
And the heat would hit the nape of my neck
With the strength of blazing rays
That scorched Icarus' wings
To slowly melt the wax.

Ashiato (Footsteps)

The woodland walk is as muddy and wet as I remember.

From when I was six, Papa would take me
As a Saturday treat to Koajiro Woods
Where we would leap over logs and duck under branches,
Gripping our wellies, slippery in the mire
And head to the lake
To peek at cygnets timidly taking to water, or
Wonder at tadpoles sprouting their tiny limbs
Before heading home to scoff *oyakodon* for tea.

I would always walk behind Papa.

His broad frame towered closely ahead,
Shielding me from *kami-san* whips of wind
And rain that lashed at my face.
Fawn-like, I would plant my knock-kneed pins in his giant tracks,
Great pools that reflected a stormy sky,
As we navigated streams and stiles. Together.
When my little legs tired,
I climbed aboard his back and pointed the path with
Sticks we had found.

In nineteen years, the woodland path has little changed her course.
Yet ahead of me, Papa's back travels slower now –
Curving forwards, shoulders stooped
And a *tsueh* keeps him steady.
I hover closely behind,
Still marking his footprints with mine,
With steps both wider and longer -
Marking, now, to catch any slip back or fall
As we slowly make our way home.

While measured of speed, he still leads the way:
So the shepherd, though weary, still tends to his lamb.

hitsujikai, tsukareni kakawarazu, kohitsuji no sewa o suru

Tamiko read Latin and French at New College, Oxford. She was the winner of the BBC Radio 3 carol competition 2021.

Acknowledgements:

Red, for the opportunity to publish my poems;

my family and friends, for their love and support; and

readers of poetry, who have taken an interest in my work.

Printed in Great Britain
by Amazon

17029085R00031